Plants

Leaves

Patricia Whitehouse

Heinemann Library
Chicago, Illinois

www.heinemannraintree.com
Visit our website to find out
more information about
Heinemann-Raintree books.

To order:

☎ Phone 888-454-2279

💻 Visit www.heinemannraintree.com
to browse our catalog and order online.

Edited by Adrian Vigliano and Harriet Milles
Designed by Joanna Hinton Malivoire
Picture research by Elizabeth Alexander
Originated by Heinemann Library
Printed in China by South China Printing Company Ltd.

13 12 11 10 09
10 9 8 7 6 5 4 3 2

Library of Congress Cataloging-in-Publication Data
Whitehouse, Patricia, 1958-
    Leaves / Patricia Whitehouse.
        p. cm. — (Plants)
Includes index.
Summary: A basic introduction to leaves, describing their
physical characteristics, function, and uses.
    ISBN 978 1 4109 3475 8 (HC), 978 1 4109 3480 2 (Pbk.)
    1. Leaves—Juvenile literature. [1. Leaves.] I. Title. II.
Plants
(Des Plaines, Ill.)
    QK649 .W45 2002
    581.4′8—dc21
                                    2001003650

Acknowledgments
The author and publishers are grateful to the following for
permission to reproduce copyright material: Alamy pp. **4, 23**
(© Phil Degginger), **12** (© Darren Matthews), **13** (© Graham
Oliver), **19** (© Ashley Cooper); Corbis pp. **5**
(© Craig Tuttle), **8** (© Günter Rossenbach/zefa), **18**
(© Bloomimage); naturepl.com pp. **6, 23** (Aflo), **9** (Jack
Dykinga), **21** (Ashok Jain); Photolibrary pp. **11, 23** (Stefan
Mokrzecki), **16** (Botanica/Eberhart Wally); Shutterstock
pp. **7, 23** (© Georgy Markov), **10** (© Filipe B. Varela), **14**
(© photobank.ch), **15** (© Hannamariah), **17** (© Peter Igel), **20**
(© markrhiggins).

Cover photograph of autumn leaves reproduced with
permission of Getty Images/Robert Harding World Imagery/
John Miller. Back cover photograph of a plant stem reproduced
with permission of Shutterstock (© Georgy Markov), and a
plant seed, Shutterstock (© Filipe B. Varela).

We would like to thank Louise Spilsbury for her invaluable
help in the preparation of this book.

Every effort has been made to contact copyright holders of
any material reproduced in this book. Any omissions will
be rectified in subsequent printings if notice is given to the
publisher.

Contents

Some words are shown in bold, **like this**. You can find them in the Glossary on page 23.

What Are the Parts of a Plant?

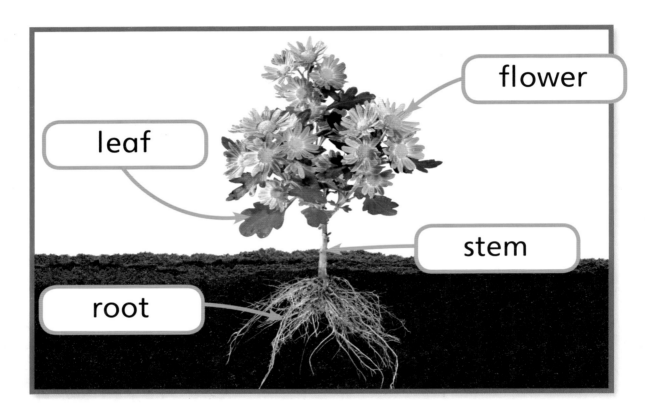

flower

leaf

stem

root

There are many different kinds of plants.

All plants are made up of the same parts.

Some plant parts grow below the ground in the soil.

Leaves grow above the ground in the light.

What Are Leaves?

branch

Leaves are an important plant part.

Leaves grow on the **branches** of trees.

stem

leaf

Leaves grow on the **stems** of other plants.

Leaves grow on the stems of climbing plants.

Why Do Plants Have Leaves?

Leaves make food for plants.

Leaves use water, air, and sunlight to make the food.

tubes

Plant **roots** take in water from the soil.

Water travels up the plant **stem** and into tubes in the leaves.

Where Do Leaves Come From?

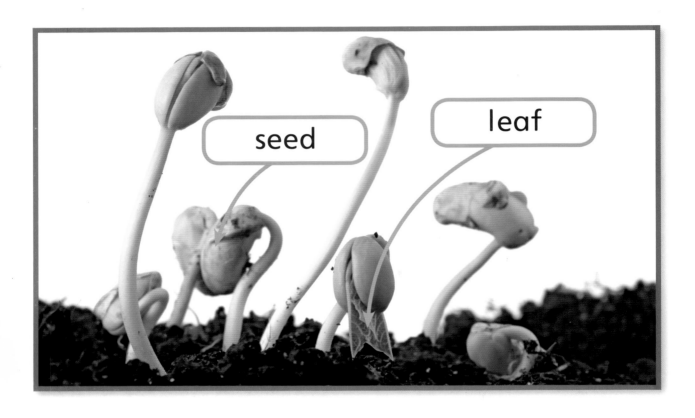

seed

leaf

Leaves begin inside **seeds**.

You can see tiny leaves inside these seeds.

The seeds grow into plants.

Leaves open and grow on the plant stem.

How Big Are Leaves?

Leaves come in many sizes.

Some leaves are so small they can fit on your finger.

Some leaves are as big as your hand.

Some leaves are almost as big as
a whole person!

How Many Leaves Can Plants Have?

Some plants have only a few leaves.

These tulips have just three or four leaves on each plant.

Some plants have hundreds of leaves.

Look at all the leaves growing on these bushes.

What Colors Are Leaves?

Most leaves are green.

Some leaves are red or purple.
Some can have stripes or dots.

In some places, leaves change color in the fall.

The leaves can turn red or gold.

How Do People Use Leaves?

People use leaves for food.

When you eat lettuce, you are eating leaves.

People use leaves to make things.

This woman is making a basket from leaves.

How Do Animals Use Leaves?

Animals use leaves for food.

This koala bear is eating leaves.

Some animals use leaves to build their homes.

This birds' nest is built inside leaves.

Count and Record

This tally chart counts plants with different colored leaves in a yard. Can you do a chart like this for your school garden?

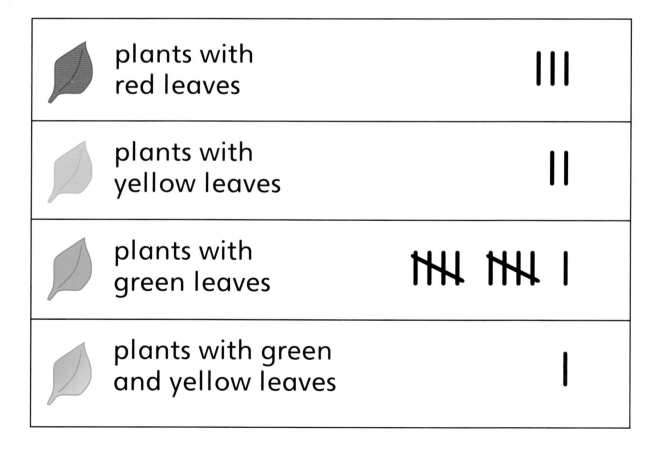

	plants with red leaves	III
	plants with yellow leaves	II
	plants with green leaves	ℍℍ ℍℍ I
	plants with green and yellow leaves	I

Glossary

 **branch** the part of a tree where the leaves grow

 **roots** the part of a plant that is underground

 **seed** the part of a plant that new plants come from

 **stem** the part of a plant where the buds, leaves, and flowers grow

Index